OFFICIAL MONEY GUIDE FOR COUPLES

CONTENTS

Creating a Plan Together	2
Managing Money	5
Tracking Expenses	13
Give Each Other Credit	18
Debt	25
Investing	34
Cost of Homeownership	45
Insurance	50
Protecting Your Joint Identity	62
Activities	66
Index	71
Resources	72

Creating a Plan Together

You make plans for the weekend, plans for your next big trip, and plans to keep both families happy during the holidays.

But plans for managing the financial details of your life together? Probably not so much.

Truth is, it's much easier for most couples not to talk about money, at least early in their life together. For one thing, it's about as far from being romantic as any conversation can be. And as compatible as two people are in most ways, there's no guarantee their ideas about how to spend and what to save will align.

That's precisely why the discussion—or more likely a series of continuing discussions—is so essential.

WHERE DO YOU START?

There's no script to follow in creating a financial plan, but there are some guidelines that can encourage candor and prevent hard feelings.

The first thing to remember is that your financial situation is unique, just as your emotional bond is. No other couple shares exactly the same attitudes about money that each of you brings to your relationship. No one will work out their differences in the same way. So while you can learn from other people's experience, your goal is to find an approach that you and your partner find equally satisfactory. Second, conflicting approaches to managing money, when they exist, don't just work themselves out. They have to be resolved.

Ideally you'll talk about money as soon as it's clear that you're serious about a life together. That means sharing your goals but at the same time recognizing that each of them has a price tag. Chances are that means some juggling will be required to reach them all. Will one of you be willing to assume full financial responsibility while the other goes back to school or starts a new business venture? Do you agree that building a savings account is more important than buying a new car? That keeping your housing costs affordable takes precedence over moving to a bigger place?

> These are big questions that get right to the heart of what's important for each of you. Once you understand one another's priorities and can agree to share in each other's goals, you will be ready to plan your financial life together.

To go forward, you need to share enough information about your individual financial situations so that each of you has a clear picture of where you are now. To be clear, it's not substantially different from sharing information about potentially serious health issues. What's particularly important is anything that could act as a drag on the future. That might include:

- Substantial debt, including student loans
- Financial responsibility for parents or siblings
- Support for children from an earlier relationship

CONTINUING THE CONVERSATION

As you settle into your new life together, laying out your goals for the future tends to take a more clearly defined path. Where is it that you want to be next year? Five years from now? Are these aspirations you share?

You should be prepared to discover that there are things that are important to one of you but not the other. You don't want to make the mistake of assuming that just because you care about something your partner will necessarily feel the same way—or that having some different goals is somehow a sign that your relationship is in trouble. What talking frankly should uncover is the goals that should take precedence, even if they require some sacrifice on both your parts.

The next step is figuring out how you will be able to achieve your major life ambitions.

That starts with a realistic sense of when it's important to reach them and what they will cost. Together those details help you create a current spending plan that includes enough saving to make progress toward your objectives.

You're likely to confront some challenges. Does realizing financial goals mean being willing to leave a job you love for one that provides more income? Or, will you agree that some things are more important to you than accumulating greater wealth?

You can't answer those questions, or others like them, without talking about them together.

MAKING DECISIONS

Will all your financial decisions be made jointly? Or will one of you consistently take the lead and the other follow? These are questions nobody but you can resolve—as long as you're both happy with the answer. But while the way responsibilities are shared—or not—isn't exclusively a financial issue, addressing it is every bit as essential as discussing your goals and your spending habits.

LOOKING AT THE NUMBERS

How important is it to have open conversations with each other about money? These statistics back up a common sense approach to communicating about finances so that they don't have a negative impact on your relationship.

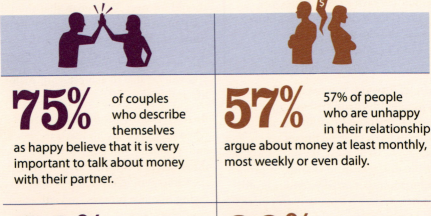

75% of couples who describe themselves as happy believe that it is very important to talk about money with their partner.

57% 57% of people who are unhappy in their relationship argue about money at least monthly, most weekly or even daily.

90% of couples who say they're in happy relationships discuss money at least once a month.

20% say that they would break up with a partner over a financial secret, like significant credit card debt, a bad credit score, or a hidden bank account.

TD Bank, Couples and Money, 2015, 2017

Managing Money

Reaching your financial goals together is only possible if you work in tandem to manage your day-to-day spending.

MAKING IT WORK

As a newly committed couple, you can live on love for a little while. But sooner or later—like the end of the month—you're going to have to pay the rent or mortgage, the credit card, utility, phone and internet bills, plus whatever else is due.

That means figuring out how you're going to match the money that's coming in with the money that's going out. That's your **cash flow**. In an ideal world, you'd work out how to manage it before you start living together. But in the real world, most couples stumble into a hit-or-miss process that has the potential to trigger some hard feelings and maybe even create a crisis.

You can avoid that scenario with a frank discussion about your shared responsibility for making sure your cash flow stays positive. And if you're spending more than you're jointly bringing in, now's the time to make a plan to reverse course. This might end up being part of a larger conversation about responsibilities and how you're sharing them. But try not to spend too much time on who is supposed to make the bed. Keep it as focused on money matters as you can.

A lot will depend on your money experience, background, and personality. If you've both been independent for several years, earning a good income and paying your bills, you're likely to have a different kind of discussion than if one or both of you have been

DURING YOUR DISCUSSION

Here are some questions you should cover, making sure to keep notes that record the answers for future reference:

Some easy questions:

- How much money do you have coming in each month?
- What are your fixed costs, which are basically all the things you have a contract to pay?
- What are the other necessities, like food and toiletries, going to cost?
- Who is going to review and pay the shared household bills? Will you divide and conquer?

And some harder ones:

- What are the things that tempt you into spending more than you probably should?
- Where will you cut back if you need to?
- How will you address the issue if one partner is not managing his or her money effectively?

chronically short of cash or have limited financial experience.

AN ONGOING CONVERSATION

Managing your money effectively is a big issue in any partnership, and not always an easy one. So you shouldn't feel pressure to get your approach resolved in a single conversation. In fact, it makes more sense to anticipate a continuing dialogue that may take a different direction as you've been together longer, or as your financial situation evolves.

Here are some of the issues that are likely to come up initially:

- If one of you earns a lot more than the other, what difference is that going to make with regards to how you spend and share recurring expenses?
- Is each of you going to contribute an equal *proportion* of your income to household expenses? Or an equal *amount*?
- Should you divide the costs, with each of you paying for specific expenses? If that's the case, how will you ensure that the division is equitable?

> Equitable doesn't always mean exactly half. It just means fair, so how you get there is different for every couple.

- Will it work better to total the expenses and divide them straight down the middle, with each of you paying your agreed-upon share?
- And if one of you doesn't have any income, what impact does that have?

While these questions—and the conversations in which they're raised—can be challenging and even uncomfortable, it's essential that you're completely upfront with each other. The last thing you want to do is agree to take on costs that you don't have the money to cover.

CHECKING ACCOUNTS: JOINT OR SEPARATE

Just as each of you probably had your own credit card when you were single or lived separately, you've probably had your own checking account. Your paycheck was deposited. You paid your bills. You used your debit card. So what do you do when you become a couple?

WORD OF WARNING:

It's a big mistake not to say what you really think, especially when it comes to managing money. You don't have to tell your partner what you think of leaving yesterday's socks on the floor. But how you feel about unpaid bills or regular overdrafts, or other financial failings that make you angry, will sooner or later fester into serious resentment.

You could:

- Keep your own accounts
- Close your individual accounts and open a joint account
- Do both: keep your existing accounts and open a joint account

There's no right way that works for everybody. Certain arrangements work well for some couples, but not for all.

Younger couples are far more likely to keep their finances separate

	Ages 18–34	Ages 35–54
Keep all money separate	38%	13%
Combine some money	31%	36%
Combine all money	31%	51%

TD Bank, Couples and Money, 2015

And whether your account is joint or individual is not a lifetime commitment. You can switch either way at any time.

Regardless of what solution works best for you, it's important for every couple to find the least expensive checking alternative that meets your needs. You'll want to be sure that the financial institution where you have your account provides the services you need and has a branch, or at least an ATM, convenient to your home or workplace.

Many banks offer what they describe as free checking, but there's usually a requirement or two. For example, you may need to maintain a minimum balance (though all the accounts in your name with the institution may qualify) or you may need to have a regular deposit, such as your paycheck, made to your account.

One complication is figuring out which decision comes first—how the bills get paid or what kind of checking accounts you have. If you've worked out a way to split your household bills, having separate checking accounts may make perfectly good sense—provided that you're both comfortable with that approach.

Similarly, if you've agreed that "what's yours is mine and what's mine is yours," a joint account is likely to suit you fine—provided that each of you spends in a way that the other sees as reasonable.

If there's just one account, it also may be easier to keep track of the money that's available and the bills that have been paid. And, should something happen to one of you, if your account has been set up with the **right of survivorship**—as most joint accounts are—the surviving owner becomes the sole owner. It would almost certainly be more complicated if you had separate accounts.

On the other hand, if your partnership falls apart, having to divide up the money in a joint account adds

IS WHAT YOU KNOW THE WAY TO GO?

While your partnership may be very different from the one your parents have, you may be influenced more than you think by the way they managed their money. If their approach was to use a joint checking account, you may think of that as the way things ought to be. The same is true if they always kept their accounts separate. And what if your partner comes from a home where things were handled differently? Can you discuss why you feel the way you do and find common ground? You may even come to the conclusion that a different way is better, even if it's not what you think of as the "right" way to do things.

another point of contention. And there's nothing to prevent one partner from draining the account, whether in anticipation of a breakup or for any reason. It may sound melodramatic, but in a worst-case situation, you could discover your account had been closed without your knowledge.

Even if there are no problems with sharing a joint account, there are good arguments to be made for a blended approach: a joint account to which each of you contributes and has access plus two individual accounts.

SEPARATE CAN BE SMART

There are several personal reasons that might make independent accounts the right decision:

- Significantly different approaches to certain kinds of spending, like gift giving
- Differing attitudes toward helping out members of your extended families
- How important it is to you to have money of your own that you can spend as you like

In addition, there may be substantive financial reasons for keeping at least some of your money in separate accounts.

THE INDEPENDENCE ISSUE

If your definition of being financially independent is synonymous with having disposable cash to do with as you wish, as it is for many people, you may feel strongly about having an individual account. And if this isn't something that matters to you, it may matter to your partner.

If your partner insists on separate accounts when you'd rather combine everything, you may feel slighted or interpret this insistence as a lack of love or trust. It's important to discuss this, and to try to keep emotions from clouding decisions that will ultimately make the most financial sense.

These include situations where one of you:

- Has a credible risk, perhaps because of your profession, of being sued or is vulnerable to a financial judgment
- Has debts or other expenses that you consider strictly your responsibility
- Has debt that could result in your assets being seized
- Owes alimony or child support to a former spouse

SAVINGS ACCOUNTS

As part of saving for your shared financial goals, short-term goals in particular, you can open joint savings accounts or **bank certificates of deposit (CDs)**. CDs are likely to pay slightly higher interest rates than regular savings accounts, which can give your balance a small boost. For example, if you're pretty sure that you'll be making a down payment on a home in six to nine months, you can choose a CD with that term.

CDs are also a good place for at least part of your **emergency fund**, the money you should have set aside to cover three to six months of expenses. And while it's possible you might forfeit interest if you withdrew your money before a CD matured, you can usually avoid that by setting up a CD ladder with three or four CDs, one maturing every six months. That way, if you needed cash in a crunch, you could be confident it would be available within a relatively short time.

Not surprisingly, the same advantages and possible drawbacks of having a joint checking account apply to a joint savings account or CD.

BUDGETING

Figuring out how you will organize your finances, and to what degree you will have combined accounts, sets the groundwork for the main tool of money management—a budget.

A practical, workable budget should be one of the products of the collaborative conversations about money that you have with your partner as you plan how to manage your money.

STARTING POINTS

Your budget is your blueprint for keeping cash flow positive, and for sticking to your saving goals.

Even if you and your partner will be paying for expenses separately, it's essential to have one overall household budget. That big picture is indispensable for having a good sense, based on actual numbers, of where the two of you stand financially, and how you

Expense Category	Anticipated Expenses
Weekly	
Household supplies	$ 65
Groceries	$ 200
Transportation	$ 80
Childcare	$ 500
Monthly	
Rent or mortgage	$ 2,500
Utilities	$ 400
Phone plan	$ 75
Loan repayments	$ 250
Car payments	$ 250
Savings	$ 400
Quarterly/annually	
Taxes	$ 3,500
Insurance	$ 750
Homeowner Association Dues	$ 200
Contribution to retirement account like an IRA	$ 1,500
Occasional	
Holiday and special occasion	$ 1,000
Medical and dental	$ 35 – $?
Veterinarian	$ 300

plan to stay on track throughout the year.

Create a spreadsheet, or use an app, to list all your anticipated monthly expenses. It can be helpful to divide them by how frequently they occur.

FIXED vs. VARIABLE

For the fixed expenses, such as rent or phone, it's easy to fill in the exact amount you know you'll have to spend. On the other hand, with the variable expenses, like groceries, there is no single exact amount. But based on what you know you spend, you should be able to estimate a fairly accurate number for most weeks.

The next step is to compare your income to your expenses. In order to achieve (and maintain) a positive cash flow, you may have to adjust some of the variable expenses—which probably means cutting back or cutting some of them out altogether. You can go back to the answers you and your partner gave when you had the conversation about what kinds of expenses would be the easiest, and the most difficult to forego.

You should revisit your budget on a regular basis. Remember, it's there to help you both, and it's not written in stone. Adjusting it if your overall household income changes is important.

SPREAD THE WEALTH

If your budget changes because you get an influx of cash, maybe from a bonus or an inheritance, you may be tempted to use it to cover increased variable expenses, like eating out, travel, or the newest phone. Certainly using some of the money that way is fine. But it's also a great opportunity to pay down debt or to increase what you're putting away in savings—either in an emergency fund, a retirement plan, or your investment portfolio.

DO

- ✓ Have a frank discussion about working together to create and maintain a positive cash flow
- ✓ Reverse course if cash flow is negative
- ✓ Work together to determine what kinds of accounts will work best: joint, separate, or a combination?
- ✓ Revisit the budget frequently

DON'T

- ✗ Try to resolve everything with a single, one-time conversation
- ✗ Make managing money part of a larger discussion about shared responsibilities
- ✗ Feel like you have to split money responsibilities the way your parents did

Tracking Expenses

It's hard enough keeping track of your own expenses.

So you shouldn't be surprised that managing money as a team effort can test your patience, especially if your partner has a different method of keeping financial records—or worse, no method at all.

In some ways it's easier for you today than it was for your parents or grandparents, who could keep track of how much they had in their checking accounts only by balancing their checkbook, which meant writing down every deposit and withdrawal, adding and subtracting along the way.

These days finding out your balance is as easy as checking your account on a mobile app, on your computer, or at the ATM.

But tracking expenses isn't about realizing that your balance is $300 less today than it was yesterday. It's knowing where the $300 went and whether that spending is in line with your plan.

TRACKING TOOLS

If you find keeping accurate track of what you spend challenging, a digital spending tracker might be helpful. Some are websites and some are apps, and they're free, though some have add-on features designed to provide more options or make them easier to use.

It's worth it to take the time to compare some of the available options. Choosing one that you're comfortable with, and that presents information in a way that makes sense to you, will make a big difference in how useful you find it.

Once you've signed up, spend some time figuring out which type of information will help you best. For example, you can usually select whether your spending is organized by category or by cash flow.

Category approach:

- Amounts you spend are allocated to different types of expenses, such as groceries or phone bill
- You get alerts when you're approaching the limit you've designated for that category

Sound like the way to go? Check out **Mvelopes** (Mvelopes.com)

Cash flow approach:

- When there's a cash infusion in your account (like your paycheck), the app automatically deducts your regular debits, such as what you'll pay for housing or internet access when those amounts are due
- Your day-to-day spending is also deducted, so you know exactly how much you have left to spend until the next pay period

Is this more your style? Look at **Wally** (wally.me)

APPs TO CHECK OUT:

- Honeydue (honeydue.com)
- Good Budget (goodbudget.com)
- Splitwise (splitwise.com)

For some people, seeing how much they're spending on clothing and shoes on a monthly basis is enough to help them slow down the shopping. For others, seeing the dollar amount available for discretionary spending is all they need to curb their spending impulses. And for some couples, the information is enough to make them realize they need to reduce large set costs, which might mean moving to a smaller apartment or leasing a less expensive car.

And though it may be a difficult conversation, comparing your spending with your partner's may be a huge step forward in getting on the same financial page. This is especially true if you're sharing household expenses, with each partner responsible for specific categories.

Probably the most controversial feature of these apps is that most, though not all, require access to your bank, credit, and investment accounts so they can pull the information they need to track your spending. In some

If sharing all of your financial information, and having it all consolidated in one place, makes you uneasy for privacy or security reasons, it may be best to stick with keeping your own manual spending records.

MESSY MONEY MOMENT

The Numbers Don't Lie

You and your partner share household expenses, paid for out of a joint checking account. You're in charge of buying groceries, and they definitely add up. But since your partner doesn't do the shopping, it's hard for him to understand where all that money is going.

To help make things clearer, you look at your spending app together, which breaks down how much you are spending at the supermarket. When he sees the number in black and white, it may make your point for you. In this potentially combative conversation, the app does the heavy lifting.

cases you can enter the information yourself, which makes sense especially if you make a lot of purchases in cash, instead of with credit or debit, which is entered automatically.

THE BUCK STOPS WITH ONE OF YOU

Setting financial goals, developing a money management strategy, and following through on your spending decisions require a joint effort. But that doesn't have to be true about tracking your expenses. When you're dividing up your household chores, you might agree that one of you should take primary responsibility for monitoring spending in your joint account, paying the bills that are due, and confirming the balance is always positive.

FIXING PROBLEMS

If it turns out that one of you, or both of you, are not following the spending plan you agreed on, what's next? Chances are it means you're spending more than you had intended to on certain types of expenses or were unrealistic about what specific things would cost.

The best first step is to rethink the amounts you've allocated to various categories. For example, if transportation costs are higher than you planned, and there's no feasible way to reduce them, can you agree to cut back what you're spending on something else? Fixed expenses are the most difficult to adjust. For example, probably the only way to reduce your rent is to move, and that involves costs of its own. But other costs that are variable, like food and entertainment, are fair game.

Worst-case scenario is that one of you is overspending and unwilling or unable to change. It's a problem you'll have to face as a couple if there's any hope of your having a healthy financial relationship and future.

PARTNER PASSWORDS

You've been warned repeatedly never to share your account passwords, but that rule doesn't apply with your partner.

MAJOR MONEY MOMENT

The Envelope, Please

It's way past time to buy a new air conditioning unit. The one you and your husband have is old, energy-inefficient and is so loud that it keeps you up at night. But it still works—technically—so you've had trouble feeling ok about shelling out the money for a new one. You suggest that you create a special savings envelope for the new air conditioner fund. You're each responsible for adding some money each week, so you decide to skip going out to lunch each day and put that money in. Your husband decides to skip a weekend trip with friends and contributes his savings to the envelope. Sooner than you think possible, you've worked together to save enough to buy a new air conditioner, and you can enjoy the end of the summer in your newly cool, quiet apartment.

Each of you must have access to your joint online bank and investment accounts, digital spending trackers, and any other financial apps you and your partner use in managing your money. That doesn't mean you're giving up your privacy. But it is one place where there can't be any secrets.

If you're looking for an electronic password keeper, Ascendo's DataVault Password Manager is a good choice because it allows you to keep passwords and other important data securely on a computer or mobile device without having the information uploaded to the cloud.

TRY THIS:

Keep a notebook (a real paper one, not a digital one) that contains all the passwords that you'll both need for financial accounts. Store it in a place where you can both access it easily, but that's not just lying around for anyone to find. This might also be a good place to keep information like the location of any bank safety deposit boxes that either of you has rented and online passwords to household accounts like utilities and cable.

DO
- ✓ Adjust your spending plan to be practical, and achieveable
- ✓ Make tracking expenses as easy as possible: Look into using an online tracking tool
- ✓ Have a safe, accessible place for sharing passwords with your partner

DON'T
- ✗ Let overspending by one—or both—of you continue uncorrected
- ✗ Refuse to reduce variable expenses that you could actually do without
- ✗ Postpone building an emergency fund

Give Each Other Credit

Using credit responsibly can be a challenge—especially when there are two people involved.

Even if you and your spouse or partner are totally compatible in other ways, you may have very different attitudes towards using credit.

You may tend to put practically every purchase on your credit card. There are benefits to that approach: you know exactly where your money went every month. And it's a hassle to constantly be going to an ATM. You may have even been hit with overdraft debit fees that you want to avoid going forward.

Your partner, on the other hand, may be a believer in paying cash whenever possible and hates the idea of running up a big credit card bill every month—even if paying it off in full is no problem.

Credit is one of those key places where you want to avoid an ongoing debate that could escalate into a major point of contention. If it seems unrealistic for one of you to change your approach to using credit (and it probably is), you should each have your own credit card.

You still have to keep your spending within the guidelines you've agreed upon. And, you each have to take responsibility for paying your own card's balance when it's due. If one of you regularly overspends, though, sooner or later you'll have to confront that together.

TWO IS BETTER THAN ONE

The other advantage of each person in a couple having his or her own card

MESSY MONEY MOMENT
A Friend in Need

Your good friend, whom you've known since you roomed together in college, has had a rough few years financially and now he's in debt over his head. His credit cards have been cut off, and he suggests that maybe you could be his co-signer on a new credit card, so that he'll have some way to start paying his bills.

You feel like helping him out is the right thing to do, but you know your wife won't agree. For starters, she's always very cautious about using credit. And you've been trying to put together a down payment on a house, so you really shouldn't risk taking on any debt. Dreading the conversation, you agree to be a co-signer on the card without consulting her.

Not surprisingly, your friend quickly has a huge balance due on the credit card—and you're financially responsible. Instead of having that money free to buy a house, it's going to paying off your friend's ballooning debt. Aside from the unnecessary financial burden, you've also broken some of the key rules of fair engagement when it comes to a shared financial life with your partner.

is that each of you builds your own credit history.

Having two separate credit histories is critical for a number of reasons:

1. Two people with strong credit histories are in a better position to qualify for a major loan, like the mortgage loan you'll probably need to buy a home.

2. If one person in a marriage has a stronger credit history than the other, that person can be the primary applicant on major credit purchases, whether it's essentials like furniture or a splurge like a second car.

3. Each of you is dependent on your own credit history to land a job, buy insurance, or any of the other things where being creditworthy is a factor in the decision-making process.

4. If you find yourself single again, for whatever reason, you'll have an established history of responsible spending that will make it easier to obtain and manage future credit on your own.

5. If one of you loses your card or it's stolen, the other person's card remains available for use until the missing card is replaced.

SHARING CREDIT CARDS

There are alternatives to having separate credit cards. One option is to apply jointly for a card, which will be issued in both your names. You're both responsible for the total debt on the card, regardless of who made the purchase. When the card's monthly balances and payment history are reported to credit reporting agencies it impacts both of your histories.

A jointly held credit card may be ideal as the card you use for shared household expenses that are paid from a joint bank account, if that's the way you've decided to organize your finances.

The third option is for one of you to be an authorized user on the other's card. In that case, you would request a second card for your partner, or vice versa. The thing to keep in mind is that you, as the account holder, are responsible for the charges on the card, and it is your credit history, and yours only, that's affected.

The best news is that you don't have to choose among these different routes to credit. The ideal solution may be to use all three:

1. You each have your own card.
2. You also have a jointly held card.
3. Each of you is an authorized user on a card in the name of the other.

NO EXCUSES: PAY ON TIME

The unbreakable rule of credit card use is that you must pay on time, even if you pay only the minimum amount due. That's usually between 1% and 3% of your outstanding balance. Of course paying only the minimum month after month is something to avoid at all costs since it increases the cost of everything you buy. (Take a look at the chart on your credit card statement to see how much more credit costs you with this approach!)

The reason it's so important to pay on time is that your payment history is the single most important factor in determining your **credit score**. That's a number between 300 and 850 that potential creditors, landlords, employers, and insurers look at for an instant read on your creditworthiness. And why is that so important? Because lenders believe that people who are creditworthy will pay back what they owe, and others will see you as trustworthy—financially and otherwise.

> If one of you doesn't take paying on time seriously, totally separate credit cards is the only possible solution.

HAVING MORE THAN ONE?

Unlike spouses, it's a good idea to have two, or maybe three or even four credit cards at the same time—each of them providing a valuable feature that differentiates it from the others. As you've probably experienced, some vendors accept only one kind of card—and some will accept several, just not the one you were planning to use.

A less obvious benefit of having more than one card is if you make purchases that you won't be able to pay off in full within the card's 21-day **grace period**. (That's the minimum period permitted by law.) Then it's smart to have a card you use only for extended repayment, and it should have the lowest annual percentage rate **(APR)** you can find.

Ideally you won't use this card again until the major purchase has been paid off. Then, even if that takes you a while, you won't be piling up finance charges on your ordinary purchases.

CAN YOU HAVE TOO MANY CARDS?

The short answer is yes. There isn't a universal tipping point when the number of cards in your wallet cascades into chaos. The better approach may be to ask yourselves how many cards the two of you need to manage your financial life.

For example, if you run your own business, act as a consultant or independent contractor, or do some other work where you have expenses and earnings, you'll want a dedicated card for related transactions so that you can keep your business and personal expenses separate.

The dangers of too many cards are very real. Most problematic is simply keeping track of the outstanding balance on each card and when the payment is due. The more cards you are trying to manage, the greater the risk of missing a payment. What's more, anyone looking at your use of credit to decide whether to extend

> **WORD OF WARNING:**
>
> Some retailers attract business by promising no interest payments on certain purchases—furniture and household appliances, for example. All you have to do is pay off the cost of the item in regular installments over the interest-free period, often a year. It's a great deal. But be careful. If you are late with a payment or miss one by accident, the promotion ends. You'll be responsible for the full finance charge.

more (or hire you, or rent you an apartment) may see multiple open credit accounts as a red flag. Too many accounts raises the spectre of the financial trouble you could be in if you were to access the full amount of credit available on multiple cards.

TIP

If you do have several credit cards, you may find that that their billing cycles coincide, so that payment is due on most or all of them within days of each other, often between the 20th and the 23rd of the month. In most cases, all you have to do is ask one or two of the card issuers—usually banks or credit unions—to adjust your billing cycle. What you're after is some payment due dates near the beginning of the month and some after the middle so you don't have to pay everything from the same paycheck.

Monday	Tuesday	Wednesday	Thursday	Friday	Saturday
				1 Pay phone Bill	2
4 Pay Hospital Bill	5 Pay Electric Bill	6 Pay House Payment	7 Pay Cable Bill	8 Pay Insurance Bill	9
11	12 Pay Car Payment	13 Pay Gas Bill	14	15 Pay Cell phone Bill	
18 Pay Doctor Bill	19	20 Pay Water Bill	21 Pay Credit Card Bill	22 Pay Dentist Bill	
	26	27	28	29	

MORE ISN'T BETTER

If either you or your partner collects credit cards, especially those offered by retail stores who dangle a 15% discount for signing up, it probably should be added to your "must discuss" list. The point is that 15% off something you don't really need is no bargain. And the more cards you have, the more you risk spending, both on purchases and on interest payments if you don't pay off the full balance.

WHOSE DEBT IS IT, ANYWAY?

You may be wondering whether you're liable for your partner's credit card debt. If you're not married, the answer is no. If you are, you may be. For example, if unpaid charges have piled up on a joint credit card or your spouse is (or was) an authorized user on your credit card, you're on the hook for the full amount. If the card is in your spouse's name but not yours you may—or may not be—responsible. It depends on where you live.

In the nine community property states—Arizona, California, Idaho, Louisiana, Nevada, New Mexico,

Texas, Washington, and Wisconsin—a married couple is responsible for the debts of either person. In the other 41 states, called common law states, one spouse is not usually responsible for the other's debt. But a creditor can force the liquidation of jointly held property.

The bottom line, though, is that to get on with your lives the debt has to be paid down, whoever is legally responsible. As with individual credit card accounts, the best first step is to stop using the card or cards with outstanding balances. That way you can make faster progress on reducing what you owe.

The nine community property states:

Arizona
California
Idaho
Louisiana
Nevada
New Mexico
Texas
Washington
Wisconsin

DO

- ✓ Get on the same page about how you're using credit
- ✓ Maintain separate credit cards if you can't agree on credit use
- ✓ Understand that you may be responsible for your spouse's credit card debt

DON'T

- ✗ Skip a payment or pay only the minimum due
- ✗ Sign up for too many cards, especially ones from retail stores
- ✗ Let irresponsible use of credit saddle you (or both of you) with a bad credit score

Debt

Debt can be one of the most daunting financial challenges that couples face.

Aside from the logistical difficulty of coming up with the money to pay off existing debt, or to stop accumulating more, debt also has an emotional aspect. For many people, the idea of being in debt is unacceptable—stressful and even embarrassing. But for others, debt is simply the collateral damage of living the way you want to live rather than the way you can actually afford. And even if you and your partner view debt in the same light, dealing with it can be fraught with discord.

Because debt can creep up on you quickly and can cause major problems—financial and personal— you owe it to your relationship to talk frankly about your views on borrowing and how you'll manage debt. It's essential to be absolutely honest with each other about how much you owe and to whom.

Not surprisingly, it would have been better to do that *before* you were a committed couple. But if you didn't do it then, you need to now. And be prepared. If one of you owes a substantial amount that the other has no idea about, the debt itself plus the fact it has been kept a secret could trigger a serious conflict.

Debt Defined: Debt is money you've borrowed and that has to be paid back, usually plus a finance charge. That charge is calculated using an interest rate that's a percentage of the principal, or the amount you owe, and the time it takes to repay. Fees may also be part of the finance charge or added separately to your outstanding debt. The more you owe, the higher the interest rate, and the longer the repayment period, the more costly your debt will be.

THE WORST KIND OF DEBT

Debt is most dangerous when it's the result of a negative cash flow. That means more money is flowing out of

MESSY MONEY MOMENT

One sure-fire way to get into debt is when you feel compelled to spend the same amount as your partner, even if he or she has more spending power or resources than you.

One Couple's Story

My husband makes more money than I do—about double, in fact. But I've never wanted to feel that I am not pulling my own weight financially. So I insist on sharing expenses that I would never choose to spend on, if the choice was mine. In addition to daily expenses like my half of the rent, I end up paying at expensive restaurants when I feel like it's my turn to pick up the bill, and help pay for trips he wants to take. I also buy him holiday and birthday gifts that are way beyond my budget, because otherwise they would seem so cheap and paltry compared to the gifts he gives me. But it's been so bad for my credit card debt that now I dread special occasions and the money I know I'll have to spend!

Solution?

If you feel like you're spending unwisely or ruining your credit just to keep up, it's time to have an honest talk with your partner. Chances are it's more important to him or her that you stay out of financial trouble, which will hurt your relationship, than for you to be paying for non-essentials that you can't really afford. Instead of paying for a high-end restaurant, maybe cook a special meal at home. And a heartfelt present doesn't need to be pricey.

your accounts every month than is coming in. Unless you work together to reduce your spending or increase your income—or better yet do both—you'll soon be in over your heads.

The warning signs of debt that apply to you as an individual hold true for a financial partnership:

- Maxing out on your credit cards, individual and joint
- Regularly making only the minimum payments due
- Skipping some payments from time to time
- Dipping regularly into your savings account to cover costs

It is true that sometimes making minimum payments or borrowing against savings is the only way you can get by at the moment. Maybe one of you has lost a job or you've had a major unexpected expense. But the more of these red flags that apply to you, the quicker you have to act to get your financial situation on firmer ground.

FINANCE CHARGES ARE A DRAG

While it's not as bad as chronic overspending, debt is a drag on your financial life when you're still paying **finance charges** on purchases you didn't need or no longer use. What old borrowing is costing you could be put to much better use if you had it available for current expenses or could be investing it for future goals. The key is to figure out a way to pay off those debts quickly. One thing that helps immensely is not putting any more charges on credit cards or lines of credit that already have outstanding balances.

DEBT'S BETTER HALF

Debt can have a good side. Using short-term debt, you can be a smart shopper, buying products you know you'll need when they're on sale or when they're available with an interest-free repayment period. But this debt maintains its position in the good category only if you always repay your outstanding credit card balance in full by the date it's due. Then debt doesn't cost you anything. As a bonus, paying on time adds a good mark to your credit history and makes it easier to get more credit.

Long-term debt can be just as good (and probably better) in terms of

WORD OF WARNING:

If either partner's approach to managing money is putting your joint financial security at risk, and he or she isn't talking about the problem, it's a sure signal that there's trouble ahead.

having a positive impact on your life together. Debt is often essential in reaching some major long-term goals that aren't affordable on your joint income, like paying for college, owning a home, or establishing a business. Especially in the case of a new business, you'll almost certainly have to take on debt to achieve the scale you need to make your company viable. In other words, access to credit can make the difference between business success and business failure.

MAJOR MONEY MOMENT
Student Loans

You have substantial school loans to pay off. And even worse than the balance you owe is the prospect of letting your partner know about the scope of the debt you're in. But you bite the bullet and let him know exactly what you owe, and what your repayment plan is.

But you didn't have anything to be nervous about—and he was relieved to finally know the whole picture of your financial stresses. You agree to tackle the debt together.

With two incomes working towards paying it down, you take a second look at your repayment plan (with some help from the repayment calculator at StudentLoans.gov) and realize that the income-based plan is a much better choice than the 10-year standard plan that you were enrolled in.

Agreeing to work together, you keep each other on track, reducing unnecessary spending as a team, and put that extra money towards extra payments. Within a shorter timeframe than you had thought, you're closer to your goal of being able to say goodbye forever to your student loan—and put your money towards things you'd really like to spend that money on, like a romantic vacation.

Even good debt has a downside. And there's no better example than the burden that college graduates feel when they've borrowed to pay tuition and other costs. About 63% say they're delaying buying a home, and, financially even more problematic, 73% say they're delaying saving for retirement until their loans are paid off.

More than 71% of the $12.73 trillion in outstanding consumer debt in the United States is attributable to mortgage and home equity loans. Another 10% is student loans. (Source: Federal Reserve Bank of New York, 2017)

BORROWING WISELY

The best way to stay away from crippling debt is to borrow wisely. As part of creating your partnership's master plan, you'll want to analyze how much you can afford to put on your credit cards each month and still pay the outstanding charges in full when they're due.

There will probably be some trial and error involved, so you need a Plan B. If you can't pay the full amount due on one of your cards, stop using it until you're back to a $0 balance. That prevents paying interest on everyday purchases and magnifying what you owe. But you don't want to stop using credit cards entirely. Charging and paying at least the minimum on time is essential to maintaining and improving your reputation for creditworthiness and the credit score that synthesizes your credit history. That's the key to obtaining future credit at a reasonable price—and a whole lot more.

Remember, it's not a solution to simply use the joint credit card you might have with your partner for those purchases you can't afford. Building up a huge balance on that card is just creating a whole new problem.

You'll also want to set limits on longer-term borrowing, whether it's how much you can afford in car payments or if you can really afford a vacation home as well as a primary residence. Teamwork may be required to stick to these limits, especially if one of you has a harder time than the other in resisting the pull of the good life.

FORESTALLING DEBT

Sadly, you can't always prevent the situations that can lead to debt. There is no guarantee that you won't be injured in an accident, you'll never lose your job, or even that your refrigerator won't stop working. If you haven't got the cash to cover such legitimate but often costly needs, you have to do something. And that often means taking on additional debt.

A better solution is being able to draw on an **emergency fund**. That's an easily accessible savings or investment account with a balance of at least three to six months worth of living expenses for both of you that you keep specifically for real emergencies.

You can start building the fund as soon as you're a couple, or combine the funds each of you had separately. Figure out the balance you want to accumulate, and then allocate as much as you can each month until you reach your goal. Then each time you take money out, add enough to bring it back to full.

At least part of your emergency fund should be in certificates of deposit (CDs) or US Treasury bills so that you could access the balance at any time with little or no loss of value. If you're reluctant to leave a lot of money in low-paying accounts, you might put some in a balanced or equity income mutual fund or in stocks whose value tends to be able to weather a modest economic downturn. These stocks, known as blue chips, are issued by some of the largest and best-known US companies.

A PRACTICAL APPROACH TO REPAYMENT

> Avoiding unnecessary debt is only half the story. You also have to work together on how you'll pay off the debt each of you brings to the partnership plus the debt you accumulate together.

If both of you have debt and income of your own, one alternative is for each of you to take responsibility for your own prior obligations. Unless one of you has co-signed a loan for the other, your creditors can't go after your partner's assets, nor can your partner's creditors go after yours. But if you have a joint bank account or own other assets together, one partner's creditors may be able to seize that jointly held property to settle his or her obligation.

The other approach is to consider all debt, old and new, a mutual obligation and use money from your joint account to repay it. True, it might mean postponing some of your goals, but recognizing that you're dealing with the bad as well as the good together may help you forge a stronger bond.

HOW LONG 'TIL WE GET THERE?

What's an appropriate time frame for debt repayment? It depends on the kind of debt you're talking about. Credit card debt, which tends to have higher interest rates than long-term debt, should almost always be paid off as fast as humanly possible. If you have outstanding debt on two or more cards, it's smart to pay down the one with the highest rate first and then go on to the next highest (while always making at least the minimum payment due on all of them).

Long-term debt may be a different story. If you have a long-term fixed rate mortgage whose interest rate is lower than the rate that's currently being offered, you may gain very little, financially speaking, by taxing your budget to pay it off faster. The same is true for a federal student loan with a fixed ten-year term. It's worth the time to find an online calculator that will help you weigh the costs of faster payment against the benefits. For example, you might come out ahead by investing the money you'd have to use to prepay a loan. One

thing you don't want to do is rely on your intuition to tell you what to do. Check the math.

CHOOSE A CALCULATOR

A repayment calculator can help you get a handle on what you owe on different types of loans, and how long it will take you to repay the full amount.

> Seeing this information in black and white is essential to creating an overall financial plan. It's also helpful to have the actual numbers to look at when discussing outstanding debt with your partner.

Some sites that offer calculators that you may find helpful include:

Bankrate.com

This site offers useful calculators across all aspects of your financial life, including mortgage repayments and how large a mortgage you can afford, credit card repayments, student loans, and compounding on savings.

FinAid.org

This calculator estimates the size of your monthly loan payments, as well as the annual salary you'll need to be able to handle the payments. The calculator works for Federal loans, including Perkins, PLUS, and Stafford loans, as well as private student loans.

StudentLoans.gov

The Repayment Estimator is a very helpful tool, coming straight from the source on Federal Loans. The site also offers comprehensive information on all aspects of financial aid and loans. (You will need to log in to access the calculators.)

CreditKarma.com

While this site does serve up ads and suggested companies, feel free to ignore the paid-for content and links and just use the calculators. There are ones for mortgages, auto, college, and even small business loans.

WORD OF WARNING:

If you co-sign a loan, you are responsible for the full amount of the outstanding debt if the primary borrower doesn't pay. That obligation may persist even if he or she dies or if you divorce.

THE DEBT IRONY

What would happen if you were vigilant in avoiding debt? You could cut up your credit cards and use only a debit card or cash. You could save regularly to accumulate the total price of a new car before you bought it. You could rent rather than buy your home—which you might do anyway for any number of reasons.

But you might end up regretting it. That's because if you don't use credit, you have no credit history. Without a credit history, it can be difficult to borrow, since a lender has no evidence that you're likely to repay. It can also be difficult to rent an apartment, buy insurance, or secure a job.

That seems counterintuitive, but the irony of debt is that you need to use it to establish a reputation for handling your financial life responsibly.

Yet, at the same time, having too much debt can keep from qualifying for the debt you need to pursue your next goal.

THE LAST WORD

Pretending there's no debt won't make it go away. Neither will postponing the conversation about how to pay it off. In fact, the longer you try to ignore debt the more costly it grows, both financially and emotionally.

DO

- ✓ Discuss your attitudes towards debt, and your plan for avoiding or reducing it
- ✓ Be honest with your partner about debt you already have
- ✓ Know what kinds of debt—and how much—your partner brings to the relationship

DON'T

- ✗ Continually spend more than you can repay
- ✗ Allow yourself to be in the dark about your partner's debts
- ✗ Try to pay off long-term debt more quickly than is financially beneficial
- ✗ Stop using credit cards entirely, as this can hurt your credit history

Investing

Investing may not be at the top of your to-do list. But if you're committed to building a secure financial life with your partner, it needs to be a part of your plan.

Even if it's not the most fun you ever have as a couple, it can be one of the most rewarding things you do together. That's because investing is all about enabling your financial goals—and your life goals.

INVESTING BASICS

One of you may have more investing experience than the other, or you both may be approaching it with fresh eyes. Either way, it's not a bad idea to

> If one of you is very knowledgeable about investing, or is motivated to devote time and energy to managing your joint investment portfolio, that person should take the lead, as long as you're both comfortable with that.
>
> However, it would be a real mistake for the other partner to remain completely uninvolved and uninformed. At the very least, both partners should have access to your account statement, and be involved in review of investments, approaches, and financial goals at least once a year. This might occur in a meeting with a financial adviser, if you're working with one.

get on the same page about what the basics entail.

Investing is about buying assets that you expect to increase in value, provide income, or, in some cases, do both. These assets aren't houses or cars. Usually they're stocks, bonds, or the mutual funds or exchange traded funds (ETFs) that invest in stocks and bonds.

INVESTING OPTIONS

Corporations issue stocks and bonds. Governments issue bonds. In both cases, it's because they need capital, meaning money, to keep running or to expand. Instead of going to a bank, as you probably will if you need to borrow to buy a house, the issuers prefer to raise capital from investors, attracting them by offering something of value in exchange for the capital.

With **stocks**, the value is an ownership share in the corporation. With **bonds**, it's the promise of your money back plus interest at a specific point in the future.

What you expect, when you invest in one or more stocks or in a mutual fund or ETF that invests in stocks, in that the stocks' prices will go up over time and, in some cases, that the corporation will pay investors a share of its profits, called a dividend. Or, if you buy a bond, you expect interest income each year until the bond's term ends and then repayment of the principal.

> Stocks and bonds are sometimes referred to as **securities**, while mutual funds and ETFs may be called **investment products**. You can buy individual stocks and bonds through a brokerage account, or you can buy a group of stocks and bonds indirectly by choosing a mutual fund or ETF that has put together a portfolio, or group, of stocks or bonds to meet a specific investment objective like growth or income.

Over time, it works. People have made more money owning stocks, bonds, mutual funds, and ETFs than they would have by keeping their money in savings accounts or CDs. But investments are not insured the way savings are. You may not earn as much as you expected, and it's also possible that you could lose some—or in an extreme case, all—of the money you invested.

The fear of that risk of losing money is one hurdle that all investors—not just novice ones—need to conquer.

> What can make that fear even greater when investing jointly is that you may feel responsible to your partner if an investment you picked doesn't do well. But no investors—even professionals—make the right investment decisions all the time. The key is to invest knowledgeably, and with an eye to the long-term. The worst mistake would be not investing at all.

RISK AND RETURN

The truth is that when you invest you have to take a certain amount of **risk**. It's the only way to get the return you need to stay ahead of inflation or provide the money you need to meet the big financial goals you and your partner share. In fact, there's a direct relationship between risk and return.

What's **investment return**? It's the combination of change in an asset's value (up or down) plus any income the asset provided over a specific period, often a year. You can state it as a dollar amount or as a percentage of the amount you invested. The bigger the return, the better.

Taking risk doesn't mean being buying wildly and without a strategy in place. Strong investment return also depends on making smart choices about where you put your money. It takes time and energy to figure out where that is. This is a case where both of you working together, each doing some research and reading and then sharing what you've learned, can make the task a little more approachable. For example, if you know you want to diversify your portfolio by adding some investments in sustainable energy, you'll need to research the best option, which includes reading the investment prospectus and looking at the investment's track record.

> An investor's tolerance for risk is a defining feature that deeply influences his or her approach to investing—as well as the success of his or her investment portfolio. When you're investing as a twosome, it's going to be difficult to invest together unless you have compatible approaches to investment risk. Compromise may be the order of the day, to reach a risk profile that you are equally comfortable with.

In a worst-case scenario, incompatibility about risk could mean you don't invest at all, which will make it virtually impossible to create a strong financial life, and future, together. A better alternative is to agree to split the money you're allocating to investing into two equal piles, enabling each of you to invest in the way that you're comfortable.

FOR BETTER OR WORSE

The other thing you have to remind each other about investing is that it is a long-term proposition. That's because investments, stock investments in particular, tend to be volatile. That means their value, as measured by their market price, can change quickly and sometimes dramatically. If you panic and sell for less than you paid, you lock in your loss. But if you hold on to a stock or fund despite a drop in its price, you give the investment the chance to recover and perhaps gain more than it lost. That's why younger investors can afford to take more risk—your portfolio has many more years to recover from any losses.

> It may be hard to commit to putting that money into investments rather than using it for fun things like clothes, eating out, and travel. And nobody's saying you need to give those things up entirely. But the only way to create financial security for your future is to invest.

START NOW, START SMALL

You should also think of investing as a long-term proposition because the sooner you start, the greater the potential for building a substantial portfolio—provided you reinvest all the dividends and interest you earn. Though it might seem hard to believe, waiting even ten more years to start investing could mean the difference of hundreds of thousands of dollars.

The first step is to make sure you have an emergency fund you can draw on in case something goes wrong in your financial life. What you want is six months of living expenses stored in a relatively risk-free account, like a CD or US Treasury bills. Then if one of you is injured in an accident or gets sick and can't work, there's money to help pay the bills. The fund can also be a lifesaver if one of you is between jobs, you have to rebuild your home, or help out a family member.

When you've reached your dollar goal for the fund, you can repurpose the money you've been using to build it to make investments instead. Starting small is just fine, and you can learn as you go. You can open most mutual funds with less than $5,000, sometimes much less, and add $100 a week or whatever amount you're willing to commit. If you set up a direct deposit from your checking account or have your employer deposit the investment amount directly in your mutual fund or brokerage account, you're off and running.

Just like with your bank accounts and credit cards, you'll have to decide whether you should own your investment accounts jointly or if each of you should have your own accounts. There are good arguments for either approach if you're married. Or you may decide on a blended approach, keeping investments you already own in your own names and making new investments in a joint account.

If you're not married, it may make more sense to choose individual accounts, at least for now. Should you have to divide up your assets down the road, having separate investment accounts will remove one potential challenge.

DON'T WAIT

One thing you don't have to do is wait until you pay off your student loans—if you have them—before you start investing. As long as your return is higher than the interest rate you're paying on the loans, you may be able to come out ahead by investing what you can. That's even truer if you qualify to deduct the interest you're paying on the loans when you file your tax return each year.

MAKING INVESTMENTS

You make investments one of two ways. You open a brokerage account and do your buying and selling through that account. Or, in the case of certain mutual funds, you open an account with the investment company offering the funds and buy and sell directly with the company.

To open a brokerage account, you can either visit an office of the brokerage firm with which you plan to work, or, more conveniently, you can go to the firm's website and open an online account. When you give an order to buy or sell a specific investment, you authorize your firm to act on your behalf, following your instructions.

There is a cost when you use a brokerage account, but if you shop around it shouldn't be hard to find a firm with low fees and a strong reputation for customer service.

ROBO-ADVISORS

Not having a lot of money to invest can make it intimidating, or even impossible, to start a relationship with a broker or investment advisor.

One approach, if this is a reason that you might be putting off investing, is to try a robo-advisor. With low fees and a low (or non-existent) minimum to open an account, a robo-advisor is an automated online platform that uses algorithms, based on your financial profile, to create and manage a personalized investment plan, including retirement plans, taxable plans, and college savings plans. The plans are goals-based and take your risk tolerance into account, just as a financial advisor would do.

Wealthfront and **Betterment** are two of the most highly rated options, and others worth investigating are **Ellevest**, which factors in investment challenges specific to women, including longer lifespans and lower salaries, and **WealthSimple**, which offers Socially Responsible Investing (SRI) options.

ASSET ALLOCATION

Asset allocation means you spread your investment principal across the major asset classes: equity, which includes stocks and stock funds, debt, which includes bonds and bond

INVESTMENT STRATEGIES

Investing is not a decision-by-the-seat-of-your-pants activity. Instead, you need a strategic, methodical approach that includes:

- Allocating your assets
- Diversifying within asset classes
- Identifying specific investments to buy
- Monitoring investment performance
- Establishing guidelines for selling

funds, and cash equivalents, which include CDs and US Treasury bills. The reason allocation is important is that each of these classes has ups and downs, but they tend to operate on different cycles. So when stocks are providing stronger than average returns, bonds may be providing weaker ones. Then, sometimes rather quickly, the tables can turn, and bond return can be stronger and stock return weaker.

Having a percentage of your total principal in each class means you're always in a position to benefit from whichever class is doing better. There are some rules of thumb about what those percentages could be, such as 60-30-10, or 60% in equity, 30% in debt, and 10% in cash. The younger you are, and the more risk you're willing to take, the larger your allocation to equities probably should be.

But it's also essential to remember that while asset allocation can benefit overall performance and help you manage risk, it doesn't guarantee a positive return or protect against losses in a falling market.

DIVERSIFICATION

Diversifying within asset classes means being sure you own a variety of stocks and a variety of bonds, not just one or two. For most people, including young couples, the easiest way to diversify is to invest in mutual funds and ETFs that are already diversified. For example, if you invest in an ETF tracking the S&P 500 stock index, you're invested indirectly in 500 large-company US stocks. If you invest in a total US bond index fund, you're invested indirectly in thousands of bonds.

Diversification helps you manage the risk that the value of stocks or bonds that you own might drop in value, or a stock may cut its dividend. But, as with asset allocation, while this strategy can boost return and moderate risk, it doesn't guarantee a positive return or protect against losses in a falling market.

You also need to develop a strategy for buying new investments, keeping track of the way your investments are performing, and getting rid of investments that no longer meet your expectations. Identifying what to buy and when to sell are skills you'll need to develop as a team, though here too you can simplify the process by concentrating on mutual funds and ETFs while you learn more about investing. With funds, buy and sell decisions are made for you.

Tracking performance is a lot easier. What you do is identify the market index that is the appropriate benchmark for your investment. In fact, an actively managed mutual fund tells you in its prospectus what that benchmark is. If your return is higher than the index, you can consider the performance positive. And if you buy index mutual funds and ETFs, which own the same investments that the index they follow owns, the performance of your investments should be nearly identical to the benchmark.

The more experience you develop, the more skill you can put to work allocating, diversifying, evaluating, and updating across your accounts.

INVESTING TO MAKE A DIFFERENCE

Increasingly, in addition to investing as a way to meet long-term financial goals, people are looking for ways to make sure that their investment dollars are also working to make a positive impact in the world, helping combat economic, social, or environmental problems.

If you and your partner agree to invest this way, you can select the stocks or bonds of individual companies that meet specific environmental, social, or corporate governance criteria. Or, more commonly, you can choose among roughly 500 mutual funds or ETFs whose investment objectives are aligned with your values.

Most mainstream investment companies offer ETFs and mutual funds that invest solely in companies that meet certain standards for environmental responsibility and sustainability, or that support specific communities. As in your other investment research, prospectuses and company websites are a great place to start your research.

WORKING WITH A PROFESSIONAL

One way to learn more about investing while benefiting from professional advice is to work with a stockbroker or investment adviser on a plan for investing. Finding the right professional can be a challenge because you're looking for a sometimes elusive combination of knowledge, experience, and compatibility. You can start by asking your families, your friends, and your other professional advisers, such as your lawyer or accountant, for recommendations. Or you may want to check out the financial consultants available through your bank.

One big advantage of working with an adviser is that he or she can help you see all your individual, joint, and retirement accounts as part of a whole. That will let you allocate and diversify

broadly, making choices about what investments should be in which accounts to take advantage of as many tax savings as you can. The less you pay in tax on investment earnings, the more money will be at work helping you realize your goals.

Both of you will want to be comfortable working with whatever adviser you end up choosing. Among other things, you should insist that he or she treats both of you as equally responsible for asking questions and making decisions.

How do you determine if you've found the right professional? Asking a few direct questions will let you know if you're on the right track, or if you need to keep looking.

1. What are your professional credentials? (For example, CFP, ChFC)
2. What's your experience working with couples like us—with similar ages, goals, and assets?
3. How do you charge for your services? Is there any flexibility with regard to fees or how you charge?
4. Do you earn fees for referrals or product sales?
5. How would you describe your investment philosophy and approach?
6. What can we expect with regard to return on our portfolio?
7. What is your recommended approach to asset allocation?
8. How often will we meet to review our investments, and how will you keep us up to date on our portfolio?

INFORMED, INVOLVED

The more effort you put into learning about investing as a couple, the more productive and empowering your consultations with your adviser are likely to be. You don't want to be told what investments to make and how your account should be managed. You want to decide.

Just be sure before you make any financial commitments to check the adviser's credentials, either at **FINRA's** BrokerCheck link at www.finra.org for brokers, at the **SEC's** www.adviserinfo.sec.gov for investment adviser firms, or with your state's securities regulator. You can find a list at www.nasaa.org/about-us/contact-us/contact-your-regulator.

INVESTING FOR RETIREMENT

If your employers offer retirement savings plans, both you and your partner should definitely participate. If you've been contributing money from your paycheck each month, you're already an investor even if you haven't been spending much time thinking about your account. This is an investment opportunity too good to pass up—especially if your employers match your contributions.

What is it that makes investing for retirement different from any other kind of investing? Taxes, withdrawal limits, and loan options all are factors:

1. Earnings on retirement investments are tax deferred. You owe no tax as they accumulate, which means that your account value compounds more quickly than a similarly invested account from which you withdraw to pay taxes.
2. Your account is portable, so if you change jobs you can either move the account value to your new employer's plan if that plan accepts transfers or roll it over into an individual retirement account (IRA).
3. You choose the investments for your account, usually from a menu of alternatives offered in your employer's plan.
4. You can track your investment performance and buy and sell in your account, just as you can in a nonretirement account. The difference is that if you sell holdings at a profit, no tax is due on your gain. But there may be transaction costs.
5. You can't withdraw from your account without owing a penalty while you're working for the employer offering the account, though you may qualify for a hardship exception. If you leave the job for any reason you can withdraw without penalty any time after you turn 59½.
6. Many but not all plans allow you take loans against your account value.

All employers who offer retirement savings plans offer the traditional tax-deferred variety. If you participate, you can defer income tax on your contributions as well as on your earnings. That reduces your taxable income, and so the income tax you owe. Then, when you withdraw from the account, which you must begin to do at 70½—actually by April 1 of the year following the year you turn

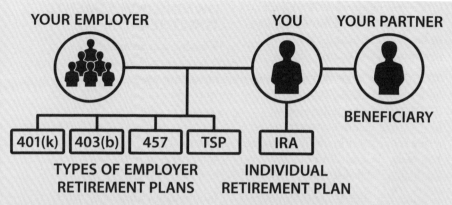

Retirement savings accounts have very unimaginative names: 401(k), 403(b), 457, and thrift savings plan (TSP). The numbers reference the section of the federal tax code that authorizes the particular type of account. All these accounts have the same annual contribution limits and catch-up contribution limits. You can move your assets from one type of plan to another in a tax-free transaction without penalty if you change employers.

70½—you owe tax on the amount you take out, at the same rate you pay on your ordinary income.

Some employers who offer traditional accounts also offer a tax-deferred Roth alternative. If you choose the Roth, you contribute after-tax income rather than pretax income, so there's no up-front tax deferral. But there are two big advantages: withdrawals are never required no matter how old you are, and no tax is due on any withdrawals you do make.

While there is no way to be sure you'll make out better long term with a Roth, it seems likely in most cases. You'll want to weigh the pros and cons with your partner and your tax and investment advisers.

Retirement savings accounts and IRAs are by definition individual accounts. You can't own them jointly. But you do have to name a beneficiary on each of these accounts, and in most cases it makes sense to name each other. In fact, if you're married, many employer plans require you to name your spouse as beneficiary. That rule doesn't apply to IRAs.

A WORD ABOUT IRAs

IRAs, like employer plans, are retirement accounts. Earnings are tax deferred, there are caps on annual contributions, and they come in two varieties: traditional and Roth. An important way in which they differ is that you set up an IRA yourself with a bank, mutual fund company, or brokerage firm and choose the investments you want.

To contribute to an IRA, you must have earned income. But if you're married and your spouse doesn't have earned income, you can set up a spousal account in his or her name. You make the contribution, and he or she makes the investment decisions.

If you're not eligible for an employer's plan or your employer doesn't offer one, an IRA is the next best thing. And, if you are participating in your employer's plan, you can contribute to an IRA anyway. It would be hard to find a good reason for not doing both.

OWNING INVESTMENTS TOGETHER

Whether you are married or not, you can own investment assets in a number of ways—separately, jointly with rights of survivorship, or as tenants in common. The way that you own the assets, as well as whether you are married or not, will affect what happens to the assets when one partner dies.

Joint tenancy means that when one owner dies, the property goes automatically to the surviving spouse. If you are not married, the value is part of the estate of the partner who has died, which means that there are potential estate and inheritance taxes.

DO
- ✓ Start to invest as soon as you can to allow your money to grow to meet your longer-term goals
- ✓ Learn the basics of investing so that you can make informed choices and decisions as a team
- ✓ Hold investments for the long-term, rather than locking in losses by selling in a downturn
- ✓ Take advantage of all forms of tax-deferred retirement account investing available to you

DON'T
- ✗ Remain completely uniformed about your investments, even if your partner takes the lead in managing your portfolio
- ✗ Let your fear of losing money mean that you don't take enough investing risk to allow your portfolio to grow
- ✗ Put off investing and miss out on the possibilities for compounding and growth

Cost of Homeownership

Buying a home together may be the next step in your relationship—one you may have looked forward to for a long time.

Owning a home, as opposed to renting, can make a lot of financial sense. You generally get more space per dollar when you buy, you can deduct your mortgage interest on up to $750,000 in mortgage debt on your tax return, and you may be able to sell at a profit when you're ready to move. It can also be a dream come true to own a home with your loved one.

But there are some potential financial traps in owning a home that can catch you unawares, and turn the dream a bit dark.

THE COSTS OF BUYING

For most people, buying a home is the largest single purchase they ever make. It's probably also the most complicated, primarily because there are so many decisions to make at every step in the process.

The first, of course, is how much you can afford. There's a fairly reliable (but not always realistic) rule of thumb to get you started: You should plan to spend no more than about 30% of your gross monthly income on housing costs. But what, exactly, are those costs?

RULE OF THUMB

Spend no more than **30%** of your gross income on housing.

Since you're more likely than not to take a mortgage loan—77% of homebuyers do—you can start with the loan principal and the interest, calculated as an annual percentage rate (APR).

So, for example, if you borrow $300,000 for 30 years with a fixed APR of 4.5%, your monthly payment would be $1,520. It's too soon to breathe a sigh of relief if that number fits your budget. If you borrow 80% or more of the price you pay for the property, you'll also have to pay private mortgage insurance (PMI), at up to 1% of the loan amount per year. At the high end, that's another $3,000 in this example, or $250 a month.

The alternative to a fixed rate, an **adjustable rate mortgage**, or **ARM**, can be a good deal if interest rates stay flat or go down. But it can be a killer if rates go up because your cost of borrowing will go up too. Before you agree to an ARM, be sure you find out what the largest possible amount you could possibly end up paying would be. Lenders will tell you, but probably only if you ask.

And there's more. Your mortgage servicer—that's the financial services company that collects your monthly mortgage payment and may or may not be the company that lent you the money—will add one-twelfth of the total annual cost of your homeowners insurance and your local property taxes to your monthly bill to hold in what's known as an escrow account. That way, the lender is sure those bills will be paid on time.

AND THERE'S MORE.

1. You have to be careful about not getting seduced into spending more than you can afford in a tight market. Bidding above the asking price occurs in desirable neighborhoods.

2. Be especially careful to plan for monthly condominium or homeowner's association charges. These may or may not be included in the estimate that mortgage lenders provide.

ESCROW

The amount you have to pay into escrow depends on what the taxes are where you live and the type of insurance you have—and it can be substantial, even huge. More problematic, there's absolutely no way to predict accurately what those costs will be in the future. The only thing you can be sure of is that they won't go down.

CLOSING THE DEAL

When you finalize the purchase, you need a big enough balance in the bank to cover the closing costs, which are additional expenses when you buy a home. You can count on needing up to 10% of the loan amount, though the cost varies by location. Potential lenders will want to know the source of that cash before signing off on your deal. They want to be sure you're not planning to borrow it.

Some of the fees included in the closing costs go to the lender, some to the municipality and state where the property is located, and a large percentage to pay for the costs of a title search and title insurance for the lender. The insurance protects the lender's interest if it should turn out that there is a prior claim on the property, fraud, or forgery that's upheld in court and negates the sale. If you want title insurance to protect your own interest, there's an additional charge.

You may also have to prepay some property taxes and insurance, which the lender will hold in an escrow account and use to pay those bills as they come due.

If you work with a real estate attorney to represent your interest in the negotiation and purchase—which you probably should do—you'll owe a fee for his or her service as well. You may also be charged for the lender's attorney.

HOMEBUYING HELP

The Consumer Financial Protection Bureau (CFPB) provides valuable information on the details of home buying, including an interactive loan estimate and a step-by-step walk through of the buying process. It's worth checking out at **www.consumerfinance.gov/owning-a-home/loan-estimate/**

MAINTAINING YOUR HOME

Mortgage payments and closing costs aren't the only costs of home ownership.

Some of the rest aren't that different from what you'd be paying in a rental, including electricity, cable, and phone. But there are others that can sneak up on you.

One of the big ones is the cost of heat and air conditioning, which, depending on where you live, could

rival the size of your mortgage payment. In an especially cold winter in an especially cold part of the country, keeping warm could decimate your budget. Not to mention air conditioning costs in a hot climate.

The other potential money trap that faces all homeowners is that maintenance and repairs are your responsibility. If you discover a leaky roof or a cracked foundation, you have to deal with it. This is a classic case of "a stitch in time saves nine"—the longer you wait to repair something structural in a home, the bigger, and more expensive, the problem will become.

Thinking of just doing it yourself? Even if you or your partner is handy with a hammer, there are some tasks that need a professional to get done right—think electrical wiring and plumbing.

Another thing to keep in mind if you're moving from an apartment to a home with outdoor space is that a lawn and driveway, though lovely, cost money to keep up. Lawn mowing, snow plowing, garbage pickup—these may be additional costs that will need to find a place in your budget.

MOVING ON

Selling your home probably won't be quite as complicated as buying it. But some potentially expensive surprises may lurk.

For starters, you can't count on getting the price you want—or what you think your home is worth. For example, when you're ready to sell, interest rates may have gone up. That limits what potential buyers can afford to pay. Your neighborhood may not be as desirable as it was when you bought. Or an unusual feature of the house that you find charming may strike other people as just plain odd.

It's not a happy thought, but it's also possible that you may not be able to sell at all within your timeframe. That could be a major financial burden, especially if you have to relocate for a new job. Some, but certainly not all, employers will help you out if you're having trouble selling. Or you might be able to find a tenant (although being a long-distance landlord has its own challenges).

Owning a home together can be a great accomplishment, and a wonderful experience. But it will go a lot more smoothly, and help you maintain your financial stability, if you take a careful look at the costs of homeownership that aren't immediately obvious.

HIDDEN COSTS

- Closing costs (10% of your mortgage)
- Real estate attorney fees
- Mortgage servicer fees
- Property taxes
- Insurance
- Homeowner association fees
- Maintenance and repairs
- Selling

Insurance

Your financial life holds risks.

One of your biggest financial risks is confronting unexpected expenses that you and your partner can't afford, no matter how careful you are with your money. That's where insurance comes in.

There is no way to predict what will happen during your life together. You may lead lucky lives without serious illness or accidents. But there is always the chance that you will have to confront a challenge that has serious financial ramifications. Having the right kind of insurance, in the right amounts, can make the difference between rising above catastrophe and being overwhelmed by it.

HEALTH INSURANCE

Health insurance isn't optional. You both need it right from the start of your relationship. Ideally your employers offer healthcare plans as part of your benefits packages—or perhaps a choice of different plans.

If each of you has an employer plan you're happy with, then it probably makes sense for you each to keep your own separate coverage.

But if you have health insurance and your partner doesn't—or the other way around—the first step is to find out if the uninsured person can be added to the insured person's policy. There's no guarantee a plan will offer partner coverage. If it does, the option may be available only for spouses, though some plans cover domestic partners. If your employer doesn't offer the kind of coverage you need, it's worth it to ask them to revise the policy.

If your employers don't offer family coverage, check out organizations to which you belong, such as alumni groups or professional organizations. One of them may offer a plan that would meet your needs. You can also investigate the individual coverage that's available from insurance companies or though the Affordable Care Act (ACA) in your state.

A MOVING TARGET

The ACA insurance marketplace is unsettled at the moment, but that doesn't mean you should postpone getting insurance. Because coverage details vary state by state and based on your situation, it's best to check out www.healthcare.gov for more information.

HOW HEALTH INSURANCE WORKS

Employers pay an annual **premium** to an insurance provider offering a specific plan or group of plans. In exchange, the provider pays the healthcare costs for people insured under the plans.

Most employers pay a percentage of the premium and you pay the balance, which is deducted from your paycheck. The good news is that this money is pre-tax dollars, so it reduces what you owe on taxes. Employers typically pay a larger share than employees do. But if you can add your partner to your plan, you are likely to be responsible for more, or all, of the premium for him or her.

The majority of health insurance plans have a **deductible**. That's the amount you have to pay yourself, out-of-pocket (OOP), before your plan will begin to pay its share of your healthcare costs. The premiums you pay to be covered don't count toward the deductible.

In most plans, preventive services, such as cancer screenings and immunizations, are covered without cost to you, but they usually don't count toward your deductible. Neither do services that your plan doesn't cover, such as things like cosmetic surgery.

If you leave a job where you've had health insurance, you may be able to continue that coverage until you're eligible for a new employer's plan. It's very expensive—typically you pay 102% of your employer's cost for the insurance. And it's not always handled effectively. But this option, called COBRA, is definitely better than not having insurance if you need medical care before you're covered under a new employer's plan.

Another option would be to move your coverage to your partner's plan, if that's allowed, until your new plan goes into effect.

TYPES OF COVERAGE

One of the big issues with health insurance, in addition to being expensive, is that it's complicated. There are multiple providers, each with several types of plans, each working differently from the others. That matters because you're likely to find yourself in a position of having to choose among alternatives. To end up with a plan that works for you means you have to understand the fine print.

Managed Care

Managed care plans have a list of participating healthcare providers. The plan negotiates fees with its providers, and your cost for each visit to a provider is set by your employer's plan. It could be a copay, which is a dollar amount, like $25, or coinsurance, which is a percentage of the total, like 10%. But if you use a provider who isn't on the plan's list, you'll be responsible for a much higher portion of the cost and maybe even the whole amount.

FFS

Fee-for-service plans allow you to use any provider you wish. Your plan will pay a percentage, often 70% or 80%, of the cost it approves for a particular service. However, the cost it approves may be less, sometimes much less, than the actual cost of the service. So you could end up owing your coinsurance plus the amount that wasn't approved.

	Managed Care	Fee-for-Service Plans
Providers	Participating Network	Any
Fees	• Premiums • Copay or Coinsurance	• Premiums • Deductible and Coinsurance

HEALTH SAVINGS ACCOUNTS

If your HDHP meets federal standards by charging at least the minimum deductible the government has set for the year, you're eligible to open a **Health Savings Account (HSA)**. You contribute and in some cases your employer may contribute as well. Contributions are tax free as are withdrawals if you use them to pay qualifying expenses, such as medicines, eyeglasses or contacts, bandages, acupuncture—it's a long list. Any amount you don't spend in a calendar year can be rolled over for use in following years.

IS HDHP RIGHT FOR YOU?

Many couples face the question of whether or not to go with an HDHP. It costs less upfront, which is appealing. And putting money in an HSA seems smart. If you're young and healthy, it may save you some money.

But you'll want to know how you'd pay big medical or hospital bills if you needed medical care and hadn't reached your deductible. And you should honestly consider whether you'd be tempted to skip seeing a doctor if you had to pay the full cost of the visit. That would defeat the whole purpose of having health insurance.

PROPERTY INSURANCE

If you have a mortgage loan, you have to insure your home. Your lender requires at least enough homeowners insurance to cover what you owe on your loan. But even if insurance weren't required, you'd want to protect what's probably your single biggest

High deductible health plans (HDHPs) are managed care plans with substantially higher deductibles than other plans but also lower premiums, sometimes much lower. The federal government sets the minimum allowable deductible each year and also the maximum amount you can be required to pay for covered services from your plan's list of preferred providers. If you reach that maximum, the plan covers the full cost of any additional qualifying expenses.

HDHPs

Preferred Providers

- Lower Premiums
- Higher Deductible

53

investment against potential damage or destruction. You'll also want your policy to cover any liability you may have if someone is injured on your property.

Your personal possessions are protected by homeowners insurance too, with coverage generally equal to a percentage of the insured value of the home. If you rent and don't need to protect the building you live in, it's smart to check out renter's insurance to cover your possessions.

And, if you own or lease a car, the state where you register it requires liability insurance in case your vehicle is involved in an accident that damages people or property. It doesn't matter who is driving the car—it's the car rather than the driver that's covered. So one policy covers you both, even if just one of you owns or leases the car.

There are ranges of insurance coverage available with most policies, and you may want more insurance than what's required by the laws in your state to protect yourself if you're sued for damages. And, unless a car you own is old and not worth much, you'll want collision insurance to cover repairs or replacement in case it's damaged.

HOW PROPERTY INSURANCE WORKS

You purchase insurance by paying the annual premium—often in monthly or quarterly installments. What it costs is determined by the value of the property you're insuring, the amount of coverage you want, and on other factors including your credit rating and the deductible you choose.

The bottom line is that the higher the deductible you have, the lower your premium will be. So you have to weigh how much you can afford to pay out of pocket if something happens to your home or car against the cost of the premium.

If you have a loss that's covered by your policy, you can file a claim with your insurer asking for money for repair or replacement. But if the claim isn't much larger than your deductible, you may decide to absorb the loss. That's because one of the other factors that determines what insurance costs you is your history of filing claims—the more you file, the higher your premium.

IF YOU DO FILE…

If you've decided to file, the more quickly you do it and the more details you can provide about the loss, the more positive the response is likely to be. Expect a claims adjuster to contact you to evaluate the damage and report back to the insurer. If you think the settlement you're offered is too low, you can appeal the adjuster's conclusions or the amount you're offered.

Remember, though, that an insurer has the upper hand, since it has the right not to renew your insurance when the current term expires.

BUYING PROPERTY INSURANCE

You can buy property insurance through an agent who offers policies from a number of insurance companies, from an agent who works exclusively with one company, or online either from a specific issuer or by choosing among a number of bids provided in response to your search.

In addition to the premium and the level of coverage it buys you, you'll want to investigate the insurer's reputation for paying claims and its financial standing as determined by a national rating agency such as A.M. Best. You can do both online.

LIFE INSURANCE

You don't have life insurance? If it's not part of your employee benefits package, you may not, and that's probably not a problem. If you don't have kids, a mortgage, or substantial

> ### *TIP*
> One thing to remember is that you may get a better deal, pricewise, if you buy all of your property insurance from the same company. If you're currently insured with different companies, it's probably worth the time to investigate consolidating. You can start by asking for quotes from the insurers you're already using if you've been satisfied with them.
>
> If you have questions about any type of insurance, you may want to consult a fee-only insurance agent. He or she doesn't sell policies, so has no vested interest in the decision you make. But the advice you get may help you decide on the coverage that's most appropriate for you as a couple.

debt that would still need to be paid if you died, you most likely don't need it. However, as half of a couple, you may want to consider whether life insurance makes sense, as it lets you provide for those who depend on you for financial security.

A life insurance policy almost always covers an individual person, not a couple. If you're each earning enough to go on living comfortably if the other dies, neither of you may need insurance yet. But if running the household depends on both your incomes, you both need insurance.

HOW LIFE INSURANCE WORKS

To buy insurance on your life, you pay an annual premium to an insurance company that promises to pay your beneficiary a specific amount of money if you die. Your agreement with the insurer is spelled out in a policy that states the face value, or amount of that payment, and name of the person or persons you've chosen to receive the payment.

The premium, or cost of the coverage, depends on the type of policy you choose, how large the face value is, how old you are, how healthy you are, and certain risk factors including whether you smoke and if you have a dangerous job or risky hobbies. Think being a pilot, or an avid scuba diver.

HOW MUCH INSURANCE?

How do you figure out how much insurance you'll need?

The idea is that your policy's face value—also known as the death benefit—will cover the immediate expenses of your death and help your partner cover the day-to-day costs of living for at least the immediate future.

The rule of thumb is that your insurance should replace seven to ten times your annual income. So you can use that as a starting point. But if you'd like to be a little more precise, you can check out a life insurance calculator, which you can find on most insurance company websites.

As helpful as a calculator is, it can't factor in your individual needs. So you'll want to modify the basic recommendation by adding money for specific needs—perhaps paying off an outstanding debt or supporting an aging parent.

It's essential, though, to weigh the cost. Your premiums have to fit your budget. If you buy a policy you can't afford, you may end up letting the policy lapse because you can't keep up the payments. In that case, the coverage ends too. The opposite problem is that you buy a too-small policy that leaves your partner's financial security at risk.

TYPES OF LIFE INSURANCE

The basic choice, when you buy life insurance, is between term insurance and permanent insurance. With both, you're covered as long as you pay the policy's premiums, and your beneficiary receives the policy's face value when you die. But there are some major differences.

Term Insurance	Permanent Insurance
Lasts for a specific length of time, or term, such as 10, 20, or 30 years, and then ends, though you may be able to renew.	Lasts for your lifetime, or, in some states, until you turn 100.
If you stop paying the premium, the policy ends, and you get nothing back.	If you stop paying the premium, the policy ends, but you get the cash surrender value back.
Generally less expensive than permanent.	Can be more costly than term.

The reason you get money back with a permanent policy is that part of each premium payment goes into a cash value account that's designed to accumulate tax-deferred earnings. Your cash surrender value is what remains of that cash value account after fees, outstanding loans, if any, and other expenses are subtracted.

A big selling point for term insurance, especially while you're young, is that a term policy's premiums are initially lower, often much lower, than the premiums on a permanent policy with the same face value. But when you renew a maturing term policy, the premiums will increase. At some future point, a term policy's premiums may be higher than the premiums on a comparable permanent policy.

WHERE TO BUY

You can buy life insurance online, directly from the insurer offering the policy, or you can work with a life insurance agent to find a policy.

Buying directly tends to be cheaper, and the younger you are, the cheaper it is. You should be able to start the process anonymously by using the forms on different insurance company sites to ask for a quote.

With some providers, a policy can be issued and activated almost immediately thanks to a process known as accelerated underwriting. But if the underwriting turns up evidence of potential health problems, a medical exam may be required. With other insurers, including some companies that also sell their policies through agents, buying online may take longer and require more paperwork.

TIP

Being healthy is a critical factor in keeping the cost of life insurance down or even qualifying for coverage at all. The argument for buying a permanent policy or being sure to renew a term policy before it expires is that you won't face significantly higher premiums or the possibility of being turned down for coverage entirely because you're no longer healthy enough to qualify.

Underwriting is the process an insurer uses to evaluate the risk you pose, decide whether to sell you a policy, and what to charge you. Accelerated underwriting is possible when you give the insurer permission to access databases that include information about you.

Buying through an agent is likely to cost more than buying online. In part that's because you're paying for the agent's time. But a good agent can provide a valuable service by evaluating your personal needs and recommending a policy that will meet them. If the agent you use sells policies from a number of companies, you'll be able to compare rates and other policy details. Some, but not all agents, may try high-pressure tactics. But since there's no shortage of agents, you can walk away and find someone more compatible.

Before you buy any policy, though, be sure to check the rating of the insurer that offers it. There's no point in buying insurance if you can't be confident that the insurer will be able to make good on its promise to pay.

DISABILITY INSURANCE

While health, property, and life insurance are all essential at some point in your relationship, the need for long-term disability insurance isn't as clear cut.

Why is it even an issue? The fact is that people are three times more likely to be disabled during their working lives than they are to die before turning 65. Or, to use a different statistic, one in four 20-year olds will be disabled and unable to work at some point before they turn 67.

On the other hand, disability insurance is expensive, especially if the policy lasts until the policyholder reaches retirement age. And most policies provide, at most, 70% of pre-disability monthly salary up to a cap, or dollar limit. It also takes time for disability payments to start—90 days is typical—after a claim has been approved. The approval itself can also be a long process.

If your employer, or your partner's, offers a relatively low-cost disability policy as part of a benefits package, it may be something you decide to do.

If your only option is an individual policy, you may want to do a careful analysis of what would happen if one of you were out of work for an extended period.

- Could you live on just one of your salaries?
- Do you have an emergency fund that would help you meet your needs?
- Do you have investment assets you could sell if it were essential?

The answers to those questions should help you decide, as a couple, whether to consider an individual disability policy for the higher earner or a policy for each of you.

MESSY MONEY MOMENT
Not a Clean Break

You've gotten a little behind on payments on your individual health insurance plan. But you don't worry, even when you get a letter from the insurance company warning you that your coverage has been suspended. You promise yourself that when you get your holiday credit card bills paid off, you'll start making payments again. You figure, what are the odds of one of us getting really sick in the next few months?

You might have gotten away with it, but then on a weekend ski trip, you hit a patch of ice and break your arm. With no insurance, your emergency room bill alone is thousands of dollars. If you had needed an orthopedic surgeon, you could have been looking at TENS of thousands of dollars.

Keeping your insurance coverage paid up and active can mean the difference between being able to deal with an accident and having it completely derail your financial wellbeing.

DO

✓ Compare your healthcare plan with your partner's, and enroll in the one that works best for you. That might mean you are each enrolled is separate plans

✓ Weigh the costs of premiums against the level of coverage you think you'll need—this goes for both property insurance and life insurance

✓ Check the ratings and reputation of any insurer before you commit to a policy

DON'T

✗ Be pressured by an insurance agent into buying a policy that doesn't make sense for your family

✗ Put off getting life insurance if you have a partner or children who are financially dependent on you

✗ Let policies lapse because you don't keep up with your payments to the insurer

Protecting Your Joint Identity

One of the most rewarding things about becoming a couple—though one that can also take some adjustment—is forging a new identity as a twosome.

You may identify as a new couple now, but that new identity, unfortunately, is just as vulnerable to theft and fraud as your own, individual identity.

You protect your joint identity in the same ways you protect it as a single person. Among the most effective defensive measures are:

- Being careful to protect your PINs and Social Security number
- Handling financial transactions only in a private, protected wifi area—never a public one
- Choosing strong passwords for online accounts and changing them periodically

The downside, when there are two of you, is that there's twice as much information, and perhaps twice as many assets, to protect. And there are now two access points, through you and through your partner.

SECURITY SUMMIT

To be sure you're safeguarding your identity effectively it makes sense to have a thorough discussion early in your relationship to discuss the approach each of you has been taking to prevent identity theft and whether there are changes that might strengthen your defenses.

You can never be too suspicious, for example, of someone who claims to be from the IRS and wants to confirm your partner's Social Security number and date of birth. Those two pieces of information alone can wreak financial havoc if they end up in the wrong hands.

Identity thieves may also contact you with upsetting (but untrue) news that your partner has been injured in an accident or even arrested. The caller claims all he (or she) needs to arrange for hospital admission or pay bail is your credit card number and security code. The scammer is counting on you being too concerned to think clearly and recognize that the request is ridiculous.

OUTSMARTING THIEVES

To preempt access to your financial data, you might decide to make all online purchases through a payment service that uses encryption software that protects your credit card or bank information. Or you might make all online purchases with the same card, so that if that information is compromised, your other accounts are still safe.

A shredder can be a great tool in the fight against fraud. They're not expensive, and using it faithfully to discard any paper with identifying information can forestall unauthorized use of your information. At the top of the "shred it!" list is the line of credit checks with your account information that some credit card companies persist in sending from time to time.

DON'T JUST ASSUME IT'S LEGIT

If you see a charge on a joint credit card that seems unusual in any way (maybe the amount, or the place where the purchase was made) or a withdrawal from a joint checking or savings account that doesn't follow your regular pattern, don't just assume your partner was responsible. Ask about it! It could be a case of theft or fraud.

CHECK YOUR CREDIT REPORT

It's also essential to check your credit reports regularly for evidence of unauthorized use of your credit accounts. That includes accounts that you didn't even open, but that may have been set up without your

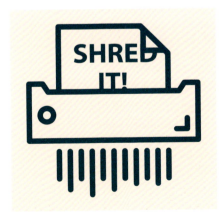

knowledge by someone who has gained access to your critical data.

Each of you can access your own reports for free three times within a twelve-month period at www.annualcreditreport.com. This gives you six views a year as a couple, or one every two months. Though that may seem quite frequent, the sooner you catch a problem, the easier it should be to resolve.

If you're using a joint credit card or each of you is an authorized user on the other's card, any misuse of those cards will show up on both of your reports.

DON'T LET LOVE BE BLIND

One of the most egregious cases of identity theft is when the perpetrator is a loved one. It happens more often than you would like to think. Because your partner has access to all the sensitive information needed to open an account, it's relatively easy for him or her to get a card in your name, and start spending.

To make matters worse, most credit card companies won't forgive the charge unless you file a police report about the theft. Filing charges against a partner (or former partner) is something that many people can't bring themselves to do, even if it means that they are responsible for paying off the debt.

ASKING PERMISSION

Though it might not approach the level of illegal identity theft, unauthorized use of your credit card by your partner is also a serious problem—not only financially, but also with regard to your relationship. You need to set clear parameters with each other about when it's okay to use the other person's credit card, including what you're buying and how much you're spending. You certainly don't want to surprise your partner with a credit card balance much larger than he or she was expecting, or prepared to cover.

Here's a list of some more measures you can take to prevent threats to your identity:

1. Carry only the credit and debit cards or other forms of ID that are absolutely necessary on a daily basis. Keep the rest in a secure place at home.

2. Monitor your bank and credit card statements regularly, checking your receipts against the details of those documents.

3. Request that your Social Security number not be used as an account number or ID. It may be a losing battle now, but there is growing recognition that Social Security numbers are used too often and for too many different reasons.

4. Don't respond to email requests for contact information, passwords, or other requests.

5. Consider using a credit card with a virtual account number security feature that generates a unique account number for each online purchase.

6. Make sure you have up-to-date antivirus software on your computer.

Activities

1. THE GOOD, THE BAD, AND THE UGLY

To get your partnership off to a healthy start, it's essential to talk about your separate financial situations and what they look like as part of an integrated picture. Try sitting down together while you create these short lists:

THE GOOD
First, list the top 3 best things about your money habits.

Some examples:

      I am a good bargain hunter.

      I have no credit card debt.

      I avoid unnecessary ATM fees.

_____

_____

_____

THE BAD
Ok, time to list 3 things that you're not so proud of.

Some examples:

      I have a lot of college (financial aid) debt.

      I tend to splurge when I see something I really want.

      I don't have any retirement investments or savings yet.

_____

_____

_____

THE UGLY

Put yourself in your partner's shoes and think about what financial fact about yourself might be of most concern. Then put it out there. (Keep in mind, many of these situations might not be totally your fault.)

Some examples:

> I anticipate having to support my parents financially as they get older.
>
> I have a terrible credit score from not paying my credit card bills.
>
> Because I work on commission, my earnings can be erratic.

_____
_____
_____
_____
_____

2. LET ME CHECK MY CALENDAR

Open your calendar or to-do app. Add one financial goal that you promise to work towards together each month. Depending on the goal, it might work best to choose a day near the beginning of the month, towards the end, or a few days throughout the month. Here are some examples:

- Don't put any new charges on a credit card with an unpaid balance
- Pay all your utility bills on time
- Instead of going out to dinner, find three free date night ideas
- Contribute to your IRA
- Meet with your financial advisor, or find one if you don't have one
- Drop one bad habit—like paying fees at an out-of-network ATM

3. SAVING WITH YOUR SWEETIE

Working together, set a savings amount for the coming week. Then write up a list of how you're going to save that money. Be creative! It's doesn't always have to be about skipping that latte.

You don't have to both have the same savings goal. It's more important to set a realistic goal for each of you. You may find that these specific ways to save are cost savings that become a permanent or ongoing part of your spending (and saving) plan.

Partner A	How/Where's Money Coming From	Amount	Did I Do It? (Y/N)
Saving 1			
Saving 2			
Saving 3			
Saving 4			
Saving 5			
Saving 6			

Partner B	How/Where's Money Coming From	Amount	Did I Do It? (Y/N)
Saving 1			
Saving 2			
Saving 3			
Saving 4			
Saving 5			
Saving 6			

4. #GOALS

Financial goals can be short-term—like a new dishwasher—or long-term, like buying a home.

Comparing your financial goals with your partner's, and seeing where they align (or not) is a great first step in reaching those goals.

1. **Separately, each make a list of your top four financial goals, ideally 2 short-term and 2 longer-term goals.**
2. **Then, make a list of what you think is on your partner's list**.
3. **Give your lists from step 1 and step 2 to your partner.**

If you were right about your partner's priorities, that's great. Even better if your list of goals had some overlap with your partner's. But if neither of these things happened, don't worry. It's a helpful step to get it all out on the table and to see where some compromises could be made.

5. IMPROVE TOGETHER

Part of being financially responsible is having some aspects of your financial life that you think could use improvement. It can be tricky if the thing to be improved is something that your partner is doing—or not doing.

While being honest about these issues is essential, it's best to try and work them out together as a team and to not let these conversations taint all of your communications about money. Just as important, be willing to bargain. Agree to change the money issue that bothers your partner in exchange for a change on his or her part.

1. **Once a quarter, choose one money issue that needs improving.**
2. **Have a mutually supportive discussion about why it needs to be improved.**

Here are some examples of money gripes that do have a negative effect on your financial life:

- Habitually paying bills late, incurring late charges. If they are credit card bills, this also can affect your credit score.
- Overspending on non-essentials that don't fit into your joint budget.
- Making expensive purchases with money from a joint account without first discussing it.

If you still haven't resolved the problem (even with the help of gentle reminders), don't tackle a new problem next quarter. Keep working on the first one until it's fixed.

TIP

When you broach the subject of a problematic money behavior with your partner, make sure it is one with real ramifications, not just something that annoys you.

An example of something that might rub you the wrong way, but isn't really damaging to your financial wellness is always making charges come out to a whole dollar, even if it means leaving a tip of $15.01.

Index

Annual percentage rate (APR)	22, 46
BUDGET	**10-12**, **16**, **48**
Fixed expenses	12, 15-16
Variable expenses	12, 16
Cash flow	5, 10, 12, 26
Checking accounts	7-9
CREDIT	**18-24**
Credit cards	20-24
Credit history	19-20, 27, 33
Credit score	21, 29
Loans	20
Credit report	63-64
DEBT	**25-33**
Credit card	27, 29, 31
Loans	29-31, 53
Repayment	32-33
Emergency fund	10, 12, 17, 30, 37
Finance charges	27
Financial planning	2-4
Financial goals	3, 15, 34, 36, 41
Grace period	22
HOMEOWNERSHIP	**45-49**
Closing costs	47
Escrow	46
Mortgage loans	46
IDENTITY THEFT	**62-65**

INSURANCE	**50-61**
Deductible	51, 53-54
Disability	59
Health	50-53
Life	55-59
Premium	51, 54, 56-58
Property	53-55
INVESTING	**34-44**
Asset allocation	39
Diversification	39
Return	36, 39
Risk	36, 40
Types of	35, 37-40
Robo-advisors	38
Investment portfolio	12, 36
Investment professionals	38, 40-42
Joint accounts	7-9, 37, 63
MANAGING MONEY	**5-12**
Sharing expenses	6-7
Retirement investing	12, 42-44
Right of survivorship	8, 44
Savings accounts	3, 10, 35
Spending plan	3, 15
Student loan repayment	28-29, 31-32, 38
Taxes	45
TRACKING EXPENSES	**13-17**
Spending trackers	13-14
Underwriting	58

Resources

BOOKS

Guide to Personal Finance
Lightbulb Press, www.lightbulbpress.com

Your Guide to Understanding Investing
Lightbulb Press, www.lightbulbpress.com

Guide to Saving for College
Lightbulb Press, www.lightbulbpress.com

WEBSITES

Educational Resources
Kiplinger.com
Mymoney.gov
Susanbeacham.com

Money Management Tools
Ascendo DataVault Password Manager (ascendo.co)
Bankrate.com
CreditKarma.com
Freecreditreport.com
Goodbudget.com
Honeydue.com
Mvelopes.com
Splitwise.com
Wally.me

Robo-Advisors
Betterment.com
Ellevest.com
WealthFront.com
WealthSimple.com

Student Loans
FinAid.org
StudentLoans.gov